W9-CMB-794

DISCARD

FIRST SCIENCE

Energy

by Kay Manolis

Consultant:
Duane Quam, M.S. Physics
Chair, Minnesota State
Academic Science Standards
Writing Committee

BELLWETHER MEDIA · MINNEAPOLIS, MN

Note to Librarians, Teachers, and Parents:

Blastoff! Readers are carefully developed by literacy experts and combine standards-based content with developmentally-appropriate text.

Level 1 provides the most support through repetition of high-frequency words, light text, predictable sentence patterns, and strong visual support.

Level 2 offers early readers a bit more challenge through varied simple sentences, increased text load, and less repetition of high frequency words.

Level 3 advances early-fluent readers toward fluency through increased text and concept load, less reliance on visuals, longer sentences, and more literary language.

Level 4 builds reading stamina by providing more text per page, increased use of punctuation, greater variation in sentence patterns, and increasingly challenging vocabulary.

Level 5 encourages children to move from "learning to read" to "reading to learn" by providing even more text, varied writing styles, and less familiar topics.

Whichever book is right for your reader, Blastoff! Readers are the perfect books to build confidence and encourage a love of reading that will last a lifetime!

This edition first published in 2008 by Bellwether Media.

No part of this publication may be reproduced in whole or in part without written permission of the publisher. For information regarding permission, write to Bellwether Media Inc., Attention: Permissions Department, Post Office Box 1C, Minnetonka, MN 55345-9998.

Library of Congress Cataloging-in-Publication Data
Manolis, Kay.
 Energy / by Kay Manolis.
  p. cm. — (Blastoff! readers. First science)
Summary: "First Science explains introductory physical science concepts about energy through real-world observation and simple scientific diagrams. Intended for students in grades three through six"—Provided by publisher.
 Includes bibliographical references and index.
 ISBN-13: 978-1-60014-096-9 (hardcover : alk. paper)
 ISBN-10: 1-60014-096-3 (hardcover : alk. paper)
 1. Force and energy—Juvenile literature. 2. Power resources—Juvenile literature. I. Title.

QC73.4.M365 2008
 531'.6–dc22

2007021057

Contents

What Is Energy?

On your marks, get set, go!
It takes energy to run a race.
You use energy whenever you
run, kick, throw, and shout.

You also use energy when you read, write, and think. In fact, everything you do uses energy. Energy lets you move, work, and grow.

The objects around you use energy
too. Clocks use energy to keep time.
Lights use energy to shine. Radios
use energy to play music.

Whenever you see a machine working or a person moving, you're seeing a form of energy called **kinetic energy**. Kinetic energy is the energy of movement.

Chemical Energy

What happens when your energy gets low? How can you get more? Everybody and everything that uses energy has to get energy from somewhere. People get most of their energy from food.

Food has energy stored inside of it. Food's stored energy is called **chemical energy**. It is a form of energy that cannot be seen in movement. When you eat, the chemical energy in food goes into your body. You can then turn it into kinetic energy.

Do you eat food from plants? Fruits
and vegetables come from plants.
Most bread and pasta are made
from a plant called wheat. All plants
get their stored energy from the sun's
light and heat. This is another form
of energy called **solar energy**.

Plants absorb solar energy and turn it into chemical energy inside their roots, leaves, stems, and fruits.

! fun fact
A few kinds of plants, such as a Venus Flytrap, get some extra energy from eating insects.

Electricity

People get energy from food. Plants get energy from the sun. What about machines? Many machines around your house use a form of energy called **electricity**. Lightbulbs, computers, and televisions all use electricity.

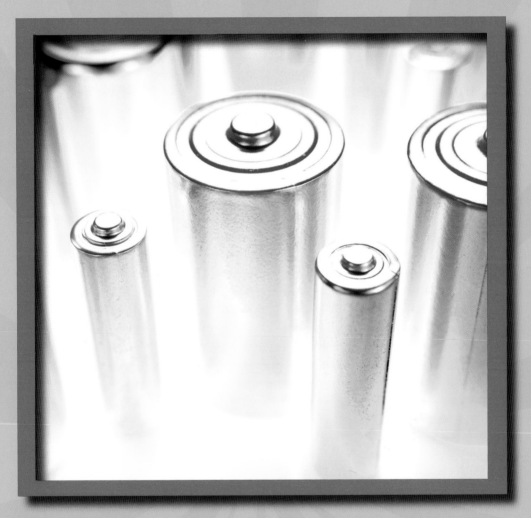

The electricity from **power plants** moves into power lines and then into your home. Most of the electricity you use is made by power plants. **Batteries** store chemical energy which can also be changed into electricity.

Power plants make electricity. Like you, they need to get energy from somewhere else. Many power plants get energy from burning **coal**. Some power plants get energy from the wind. Other power plants use **solar panels** to turn solar energy into electricity. Solar and wind energies are **renewable**. This means they never get used up, no matter how much people use them.

fun fact

Water energy was one of the first forms of energy used by people to run machines.

coal-burning power plant

Fossil Fuels

Most of the energy that runs vehicles comes from **oil**. Oil is called a **fossil fuel** because it comes from the remains of plants and animals that lived long ago. Those plants and animals held chemical energy in their bodies. They died and were buried under layers of earth. Over a very long time, they turned into fuels under the ground.

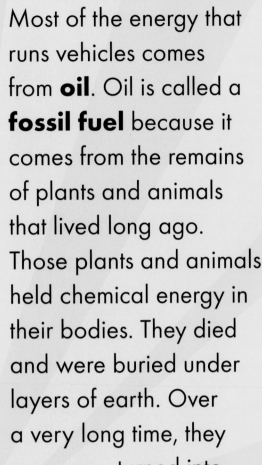

Oil

People dig wells to bring oil up from deep in the earth. Then they turn the oil into gasoline. Gasoline can be put into cars to make them run.

Fossil fuels are not renewable. This means we might run out of them.

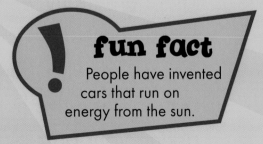

fun fact

People have invented cars that run on energy from the sun.

There are many ways to save energy.
Remember to turn off the lights or
the TV when you leave a room.
Bike to a friend's house instead of
asking your parents for a ride.

Using your body's energy is good
exercise. Plus it is fun! Let's go!

Glossary

batteries—containers with chemicals inside of them; batteries turn chemical energy into electricity.

chemical energy—stored energy in food, fossil fuels, and batteries

coal—a dark brown or black rock found in nature; coal is a fossil fuel that can be burned to make electricity.

electricity—a form of energy that makes power, heat, and light

fossil fuels—materials that can be burned to make energy; fossil fuels are formed from the remains of plants and animals buried deep in the earth.

kinetic energy—the energy of movement

oil—a liquid fossil fuel found in nature

power plant—a place where electricity is made from other sources of energy

renewable—something that can be used again and again without getting used up

solar energy—light and heat from the sun

solar panels—panels that collect energy from the sun and turn it into electricity

To Learn More

AT THE LIBRARY

Bradley, Kimberly Brubaker. *Energy Makes Things Happen*. New York: HarperCollins, 2003.

Hunter, Rebecca. *Energy*. New York: Raintree, 2001.

Weber, Rebecca. *Feel the Power: Energy All Around*. Minneapolis, Minn.: Compass Point, 2002.

ON THE WEB

Learning more about energy is as easy as 1, 2, 3.

1. Go to www.factsurfer.com

2. Enter "energy" into search box.

3. Click the "Surf" button and you will see a list of related web sites.

With factsurfer.com, finding more information is just a click away.

Index

The images in this book are reproduced through the courtesy of: Tyler Boyes, front cover; Andrew Crawford/Getty Images, p. 4; marmion, p. 5; Linda Clavel, pp. 6-7; Boden/Ledingham/Masterfile, p. 8; Joellen L. Armstrong, p. 9; Petra Silhava, pp. 10-11; Dimitri Sherman, p. 12; Mariano N. Ruiz, p. 13; Adam Marjchrzak, pp. 14-15; Phil Degginger/Alamy, p. 16; Anthony Redpath, p. 17; Ralph H. Wetmore II/Getty Images, pp. 18-19; Katharina Wittfeld, p. 20; Jeffrey Schmieg, p. 21.